Lifeboat Design and D

TYN[...]

FAST SLIPWAY LIFEBOATS

The RNLI's 47ft Tyne class fast slipway lifeboats, their design and history

Nicholas Leach

FOXGLOVE PUBLISHING

First published 2020, 2nd edition 2023

Published by
Foxglove Publishing Ltd
Foxglove House, Shute Hill,
Lichfield WS13 8DB
United Kingdom
Tel 07940 905046

ISBN 9781909540194

Typesetting/layout by
Nicholas Leach/Foxglove Publishing

LIFEBOAT BOOKS PUBLISHED BY FOXGLOVE PUBLISHING

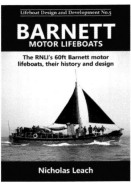

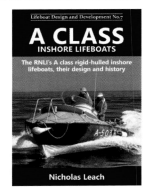

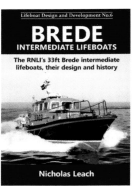

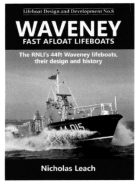

LIFEBOAT DESIGN AND DEVELOPMENT SERIES This is the fourth book in a series of concise illustrated volumes that trace the history of and describe technical aspects of RNLI motor lifeboat types. The first volume described the 70ft Clyde rescue cruisers, the second traced the history of the unique 32ft Surf motor lifeboats, and the third covered the Atlantic inshore lifeboats. Subsequent books have covered the 60ft Barnetts (No.5), the 33ft Bredes (No.6), the A class inshore lifeboats (No.7), abd the 44ft Waveneys (No.8).

THE AUTHOR Nicholas Leach has a long-standing interest in lifeboats and the lifeboat service. He has written many articles, books and papers on the subject, including a history of the origins of the lifeboat service; a comprehensive record of the RNLI's lifeboat stations in 1999, the organisation's 175th anniversary; RNLI Motor Lifeboats, a detailed history of the development of powered lifeboats; and numerous station histories, including ones covering the stations of Cromer, Longhope, Padstow, Sennen Cove, Moelfre, Weymouth and Humber. He has visited all of the lifeboat stations in the UK and Ireland, past and present. He is Editor of Ships Monthly, the international shipping magazine, and Lifeboats Past & Present, the magazine for lifeboat enthusiasts.

Contents

Acknowledgements

For assistance with this project, my thanks go to Ian Moignard for his thorough expert proof-reading and extensive comments on the text; to Martin Fish for comments and extra information; to Hayley Whiting, of the RNLI Heritage Trust for continuing to facilitate my research; to current owners of Tyne class lifeboats that have left service, notably Keith Berry, Dagfinn Aksnes and Dave Medri; and to all the volunteer crews at lifeboat stations where Tynes were operated and who allowed me on board their much-loved lifeboats. NL

Bibliography

Bailey, D. (1983): A New RNLI Lifeboat: The Tyne Class Slipway Boat (The Royal Institution of Naval Architects, pp.327-344).

Leach, Nicholas (2005): RNLI Motor Lifeboats (Landmark Publishing Limited, Ashbourne Hall, Cokayne Avenue, Ashbourne).

Morris, Jeff (2006): The Story of the Selsey Lifeboats (6th edition).

Thatcher, Keith (1992): Looking at Lifeboat: the Tyne class (The Lifeboat Vol.52, No.518, Winter 1991-92).

TYNE LIFEBOATS IN SUMMARY

Op No*	ON*	Year	Name	Builder	First station
47-001	1074	1981	City of London	Fairey Allday Marine	Selsey
47-002	1075	1982	Sam and Joan Woods	Fairey Allday Marine	Relief
47-003	1094	1984	James Burrough	Fairey Allday Marine	Padstow
47-004	1095	1985	St Cybi II (Civil Service No.40)	Fairey Marine/Osborne	Holyhead
47-005	1096	1985	Ethel Anne Measures	Fairey Allday Marine	Mumbles
47-006	1097	1985	Ruby and Arthur Reed II	Fairey Allday Marine	Cromer
47-007	1109	1985	City of Edinburgh	Fairey Allday Marine	Fraserburgh
47-008	1110	1985	Phil Mead	Fairey Allday Marine	Teesmouth
47-009	1111	1986	William Luckin	Fairey Allday Marine	Arranmore
47-010	1112	1986	RFA Sir Galahad	Wright/Osborne	Tenby
47-011	1114	1987	The Lady Rank	Wright/Osborne	Angle
47-012	1115	1987	Good Shepherd	Wright/Osborne	Relief
47-013	1116	1987	Robert and Violet	Wright/Lochin Marine	Moelfre
47-014	1117	1986	James Bibby	Fairey Allday Marine	Barrow
47-015	1120	1987	Hetty Rampton	Fairey Allday Marine	Porthdinllaen
47-016	1121	1988	Norman Salvesen	Wright/Harrison	Wick
47-017	1122	1988	Owen and Ann Aisher	Wright/Souter	Relief
47-018	1126	1987	Max Aitken III	Fairey Allday Marine	Bembridge
47-019	1127	1987	Babs and Agnes Robertson	Fairey Allday Marine	Peterhead
47-022	1130	1988	Baltic Exchange II	Wright/Lochin Marine	Salcombe
47-023	1131	1988	City of Sheffield	Wright/Souter	Whitby
47-020	1132	1987	Spirit of Lowestoft	Fairey Allday Marine	Lowestoft
47-021	1133	1987	The Famous Grouse	Fairey Allday Marine	Relief
47-024	1137	1987	Hilda Jarrett	Fairey Allday Marine	Baltimore
47-025	1138	1988	Lord Saltoun	Fairey Allday Marine	Longhope
47-026	1139	1988	Garside	Fairey Allday Marine	St Davids
47-027	1140	1988	George Gibson	Fairey Allday Marine	Appledore
47-028	1141	1989	Sir John Fisher	Wright/Marshall-Branson	Workington
47-029	1142	1989	Mariners Friend	Wright/Souter	Relief
47-030	1145	1988	David Robinson	Fairey Allday Marine	Lizard
47-031	1146	1988	Voluntary Worker	Fairey Allday Marine	Relief
47-032	1147	1988	Sir William Hillary	Fairey Allday Marine	Douglas
47-033	1151	1989	Mary Irene Millar	FBM Ltd	Portpatrick
47-034	1152	1989	Moonbeam	FBM Ltd	Montrose
47-035	1153	1989	Annie Blaker	FBM Ltd	Wicklow
47-036	1154	1989	Kenneth Thelwall II	Wright/Souter	Ramsgate
47-037	1155	1990	Sarah Emily Harrop	FBM Ltd	Lytham St Annes
47-038	1156	1989	William Street	FBM Ltd	Fleetwood
47-039	1157	1989	Alexander Coutanche	FBM Ltd	St Helier
47-040	1158	1990	Hermione Lady Colwyn	Wright/Marshall-Branson	Shoreham Harbour

* Op No is a lifeboat's operational number, denoting its length (47ft) and the number in the production cycle; ON stands for Official Number, a sequential number allocated to all lifeboats by the RNLI.

Tyne design and development

The 47ft Tyne was designed in the late 1970s as a replacement for the nine-knot Watson and Barnett displacement-hulled lifeboats for use at stations which employed slipway launching. Faster lifeboats, namely the Waveney and Arun types, had been introduced into the RNLI's fleet in the 1960s and 1970s, but these could only be kept afloat at moorings, and, as the RNLI had determined that fast lifeboats at key locations were essential to future plans, a new design of faster lifeboat was required which could operate from slipway stations. Faster lifeboats were first introduced in the 1960s, and it was initially a relatively slow process, with displacement-hulled boats still entering service in the early 1980s, in the shape of the eight-knot Rother class.

However, the programme reached a stage in 1976 where consideration was being given to future provision of faster lifeboats in areas where no suitable facilities for afloat moorings were available. Although the RNLI's preference is for lifeboats to be afloat, many locations have no

▼ The first 47ft Tyne City of London (ON.1074) on trials shortly after being built. (By courtesy of the RNLI)

suitable berth or harbour. An examination of alternative methods of shore launching was undertaken, including, in the interests of standardisation, possible use of existing classes of fast afloat lifeboats, such as the Arun, by providing them with launching trolleys or retractable launching undercarriages.

The possibility of bow- or stern-first launch and recovery was also investigated, together with the necessity for permanent boathouse structures, tipping cradles and associated turntables, but it became clear that using existing slipways and boathouses provided the most economic and reliable means of launching shore-based craft. This had the advantage of being well tried, with volunteer crews as well as RNLI staff having considerable experience of slipway operations. Housing a lifeboat also offered several benefits: the boat was protected from the elements; it was easier to inspect and maintain; and the crew can embark in the protection of the boathouse when launching.

▶ Line drawing of the first Tyne class lifeboat, 47-001. The principal characteristics of the hull design included soft, round bilges, a deep, fine bow and fairly flat stern sections. The propellers were recessed into shallow tunnels and further protected by deep bilge and centreline keels extending aft to the transom.

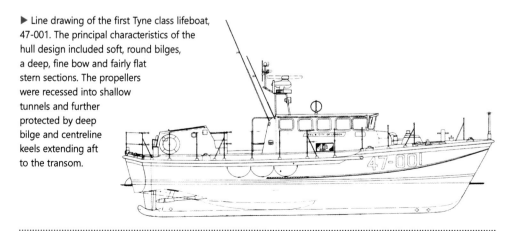

The RNLI's Search and Rescue Committee assessed these options and, by 1977, produced a specification, as well as drawing up a programme of development, which the Lifeboat Design Steering Group set out to implement. The Group included representatives of the National Maritime Institute (NMI) and members of the RNLI's operational and technical staff, all working under the chairmanship of the Boat Committee chairman, P. Denham Christie. Further groups of RNLI staff were formed to translate the outline ideas into detailed design drawings. The RNLI stipulated that the boat had to be within certain parameters so that it could fit into existing lifeboat houses: the requirements were for a boat of an overall length not exceeding 47ft 3in (14.4m), a maximum beam of 15ft (4.57m) and a height from the underside of the keel to the top of the wheelhouse of 13ft (3.96m), including a 250mm depth of keel. The displacement could not exceed twenty-four tonnes, thus ensuring that most boathouses then in service could accommodate the design.

The basic lines plan for the hull of the fast slipway lifeboat (FSB), as it was designated, was provided by the NMI. The hull was semi-planing

▲ The first 47ft Tyne, City of London (ON.1074), on trials. The small 'kick' in the sheer to accommodate the steeper deck camber and false side deck can be clearly seen. (By courtesy of the RNLI)

▶ Plating of the first of the two prototype fast slipway lifeboats having been completed, a welder works on attaching deck fittings to the deck stringer plate. The skeleton of the second prototype can be seen in the background. (By courtesy of the RNLI)

▶ The twin General Motors 8V-71 marine diesel engines, having completed bench trials, ready to be lifted into the lifeboat's engine room. (By courtesy of the RNLI)

with a shallow draught of 4ft 2in (1.27m), a long straight keel with a shallow conventional sheerline, and a flared bow above the waterline. Protection for the propellers was given by partial tunnels, substantial bilge keels, and a straight wide keel extending to the transom and ending in a hauling shoe, necessary for both slipway launching and working in shoal waters. The design of the tunnels required particular attention, as such features affected the manoeuvrability of the hull.

Once the initial hull shape had been developed, a programme of speed and seakeeping tests was undertaken. This involved model testing of the FSB design, running it in comparison with a model of the Arun class,

◀ The steel framework prior to being plated during construction of the prototype Tyne lifeboats. (By courtesy of the RNLI)

which had been produced in 1970, with seakeeping tests on both models at sea being conducted. The trials revealed a number of modifications were needed to the initial FSB design, although by the autumn of 1979 most of the significant details had been agreed and tender documents for building a prototype were prepared.

Much consideration was given to the deck and wheelhouse layout. The wheelhouse had a low profile so that the boat would fit into existing boathouses, a flying bridge amidships, and a separate cabin aft of the upper steering position intended to accommodate survivors, although in practice

◀ Recovery of the prototype 47ft Tyne, ON.1074, up the slipway at Selsey during launch and recovery trials. (By courtesy of the RNLI)

General particulars of the two prototypes

Length overall	47ft (14.32m)
Breadth moulded	15ft (4.57m)
Draught amidships	4ft 3in (1.29m)
Displacement at level trim	24.38 tonnes
Full speed	18 knots
Endurance (full speed)	238 nautical miles
Crew	6
Engines	Twin 425hp General Motors 8V-71 TI diesels

▼ On board a Tyne class lifeboat, showing the helm position and the navigation equipment as fitted when the boats were first entering service; this was modernised and updated during the boats' service lives. (By courtesy of the RNLI)

it was rarely used. The hull plating and internal structure were built from corrosion-resistant steel, with aluminium alloy for the deck and superstructure. Other materials, notably wood and glass reinforced plastic, were considered but rejected on grounds of wear, resistance and cost.

Once the specifications had been finalised and drawings completed, tendering for construction was undertaken. It was decided early in the project to order two prototype boats so that modifications made to one could be compared to the unmodified boat. The contract to build the two boats was awarded in March 1980 to the Isle of Wight-based yard of Fairey Allday Marine (East Cowes) Ltd. The two pre-production prototypes, ON.1074 and ON.1075 (later to become 47-001 and 47-002), were completed in two years, with ON.1074 being delivered in March 1982 after successfully completing self-righting and other proving trials.

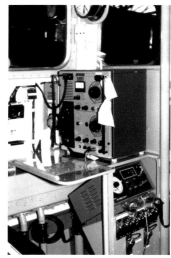

ON.1075 followed at the end of the year. Both boats were then subjected to a period of evaluation, and their performance was compared with current station lifeboats in a variety of challenging sea conditions so that the RNLI's designers could assess and refine the design where necessary. As intended, modifications were made to one boat at a time, with the two boats then running together so that the changes could be evaluated.

The evaluation period proved outstandingly successful and the alterations that were made to the prototypes were incorporated into the design for the production boats. It was decided to opt for at least two main construction yards, with Fairey Allday Marine being a prime contender and in fact the yard ended up building the majority of the boats. There were few small boatyards capable of, or willing to, build complete boats at an acceptable price. It was decided to adopt the hull part-assembly and fit-out yard concept used for the Arun class, whereby one yard would build the hull and another would fit it out.

Fairey Marine were contracted to build the first pan-assembly of hull, deck and superstructure for fitting out by William Osborne at Littlehampton, and a search was made for a second builder. The steel fabrication firm of R. Wright and Son at Foston, Derby, were contracted to build the remaining part-assemblies, and a variety of fit-out yards were

▲ The second of the Tynes, Sam and Joan Woods (ON.1075), at the head of the slipway at Selsey during launch and recovery trials. (By courtesy of the RNLI)

Cutaway drawing of 47ft Tyne

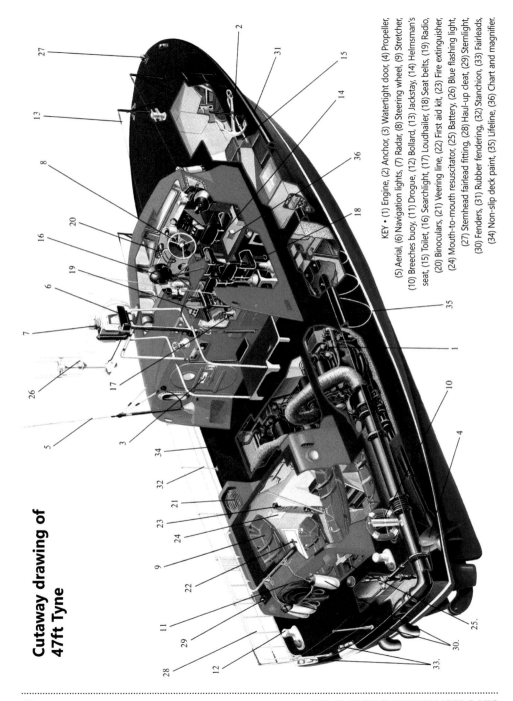

KEY • (1) Engine, (2) Anchor, (3) Watertight door, (4) Propeller, (5) Aerial, (6) Navigation lights, (7) Radar, (8) Steering wheel, (9) Stretcher, (10) Breeches buoy, (11) Drogue, (12) Bollard, (13) Jackstay, (14) Helmsman's seat, (15) Toilet, (16) Searchlight, (17) Loudhailer, (18) Seat belts, (19) Radio, (20) Binoculars, (21) Veering line, (22) First aid kit, (23) Fire extinguisher, (24) Mouth-to-mouth resuscitator, (25) Battery, (26) Blue flashing light, (27) Stemhead fairlead fitting, (28) Haul-up cleat, (29) Sternlight, (30) Fenders, (31) Rubber fendering, (32) Stanchion, (33) Fairleads, (34) Non-slip deck paint, (35) Lifeline, (36) Chart and magnifier.

TYNE FAST SLIPWAY LIFEBOATS

◀ The 24th Tyne, Hilda Jarrett (ON.1137), under construction at Fairey Allday Marine boatyard, Cowes, September 1987. Fairey, which later became FBM Ltd, was responsible for building the majority of the Tynes. (Tony Denton)

◀ The Tyne built for Workington, Sir John Fisher (ON.1141), being fitted out at Marshall Branson boatyard, Amble, March 1989. (Tony Denton)

employed. The changes made to the prototypes were incorporated into the production boats, the first of which were ordered in the early 1980s.

The hull shape of all the boats was essentially the same, but on the first two boats the deck had a step in the sheerline. Aft of this step, the deck had a heavy camber covered by a lightweight false side deck. As this was deemed an unnecessary complication, from the third boat, ON.1094, onwards, the turtle side decks were changed to flush decks. The upper steering position, which initially had only a small wheel as it was intended solely for use when the boat was being recovered up a slipway, was also enhanced, so that almost all of the boat's controls were duplicated to become a flying bridge position.

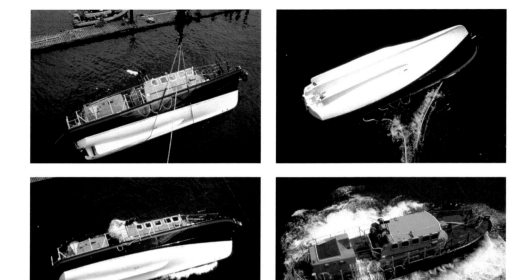

Powering the Tynes

To design a boat weighing no more than twenty-four tons in operational condition required fine control over the weight of all components. With engine room space at a premium, engines with a high power-to-size and power-to-weight ratio were needed, something that diesel engines built by General Motors offered, and which the RNLI had experience of as they were fitted in the two 50ft Thames class lifeboats. The first two Tynes were fitted with General Motors 8V-71 diesel engines.

After the 8V-71 model had been installed in the two pre-production prototypes, however, a newer model, the 425shp GM 6V-92TA, became available and so this was adopted for use in boats from ON.1094 (47-003). The TA suffix stood for turbocharged and aftercooled. Twin rudders were fitted, which were controlled by a power-assisted hydraulic system. Two main fuel tanks plus a reserve tank held 2,180 litres of usable fuel, giving the boat a range of 240 nautical miles at twelve knots or 185 nautical miles at eighteen knots. Trim planes were incorporated into the stern to enable the running trim to be altered to suit the sea conditions.

A number of changes were made as the Tyne build programme was

under way, and from The Lady Rank (ON.1114), the eleventh boat, it was decided to change the main deck material (excluding the wheelhouse structure) from aluminium alloy to steel. Fitting the aluminium alloy deck to the steel hull was difficult and involved a riveted connection at the deck-to-bulkheads and deck-to-hull joints. This was a potential source of corrosion and caused a few alignment problems. An all-steel deck offered simpler hull construction and, although increasing the weight, would simplify surveys, especially as the boats grew older.

To facilitate fitting of the superstructures, a new steel-to-aluminium alloy transition joint was used, known as 'Kelocouple'. This was a strip of material made of layers of steel, aluminium and aluminium alloy, explosively bonded. The steel deck was welded to the steel side and the aluminium alloy superstructure to the aluminium alloy side, forming a positive mechanical connection without the use of rivets or bolts.

There was also a gearbox change: the first ten boats, including the prototypes, were fitted with a standard GM gearbox, the Allison Type M20. However, as the building programme progressed, experience showed that a lighter gearbox, with a slightly improved reduction ratio, would be better. The ZF 160 BW gearbox was chosen as the most suitable alternative, and all boats from and including ON.1114 (47-011) were so fitted. The change involved a realignment of the engine beds, which could not be undertaken on earlier boats. A new gearbox from Twin Disc subsequently become available, and during the early 1990s the Allison gearbox in the earlier boats was replaced by Twin Discs during a boat's regular survey.

The various modifications resulted in extra weight and the self-righting ability of the boat was reviewed. It was found that an increase in superstructure volume would be beneficial to ensure righting ability

◀ The 1988-built Garside after her naming ceremony at St Davids on 2 June 1989. She was the twenty-sixth Tyne to be built, and the first to have the aft cabin slightly increased in volume. (Tony Denton)

▼ RFA Sir Galahad meets her Royal Fleet Auxiliary namesake off Tenby on 11 June 1988. A courtesy visit brought the then new RFA Sir Galahad to Tenby. Her predecessor was lost during the Falklands campaign, with great loss of life, when she was bombed. (By courtesy of the RNLI)

was maintained and, consequently, from ON.1139 (47-026) the aft cabin was increased in height by 125mm. The after engine room bulkhead was also moved, to increase the volume of the aft cabin. All Tynes had this modification carried out while undergoing survey.

In production

With the trials and evaluation process completed, and a production programme under way, the first boat was named City of London and allocated to Selsey, where many of the launching trials had taken place. She was placed on station in November 1983, and served the Sussex

▶ The fortieth and last of the Tynes, Hermione Lady Colwyn, on the slipway outside the lifeboat house at Shoreham Harbour on 17 September 1990, the day she arrived on station. (Nicholas Leach)

station for more than two decades. The second boat was allocated to the Relief Fleet, and the third boat, the first production Tyne, was completed in late 1984 and sent to Padstow in December of that year.

Production continued at the rate of between four and six a year until, in 1989, all the stations scheduled for Tynes had been allocated them. The last Tyne, ON.1158 (47-040), was sent to Shoreham Harbour and arrived at her station in September 1990. The Tynes proved popular with their crews and gave outstanding service: coxswains and crews became attached to the powerful boats, which gained a reputation for having excellent sea-keeping qualities, while their steel hulls were durable and the boats' weight enabled them to maintain speed in almost any conditions. At the stations from which they were operated, the Tynes achieved fine service records and were an important element in the RNLI's declared intention of operating fast lifeboats throughout the entire network.

New engines and the DDEC programme

During the 1990s a number of Tynes were re-engined to overcome problems with the original engines, which had a tendency to stall and backdrive. The backdriving caused the fuel lift pump seals to blow out, resulting in the engines being disabled. New engines were seen as the solution, so twin 500shp Detroit Diesel 6V-92TA DDEC (Detroit Diesel Electronic Control) engines were fitted to the relief Tyne Mariners

Friend (ON.1142) in 1994, which was then used for extensive trials to assess the suitability of the engines and their new control system.

The new engines were six-cylinder V-configuration, two-stroke diesel engines, which were both turbo-charged and super-charged. The engine was electronically controlled by the proprietary DDEC system. This system was designed to improve performance and reduce emissions by computer control of the fuel injection system. It engaged ahead, neutral

▲ One of the Tynes built for the Relief Fleet was 47-017, named Good Shepherd. She served as a Relief lifeboat for twenty-two years. (By courtesy of the RNLI)

◀ The first Tyne, City of London (nearest camera), with the 1988-built Voluntary Worker arriving to replace her at Selsey in February 2006. Voluntary Worker had served in the Relief Fleet for fifteen years when she was placed on station at Selsey. (John Periam, by courtesy of the RNLI)

and astern gears, and displayed and recorded engine readings and alarms. The trials with Mariners Friend proved the DDEC system and showed that the new power units eliminated the problems, while also improving fuel economy and giving the boats a slightly greater speed. However, problems with the new engine system were experienced in the late 1990s and many of the re-engined boats had to be withdrawn from service while the faults were rectified. During the production lifecycle of the DDEC engine, several different versions were produced, with the DDEC 2, 2.5 and 3 (introduced 1992) systems being used in the Tynes.

Mariners Friend had the original type DDEC engines, and these were in turn replaced in 1997 by a newer version. In 1994 the RNLI decided

Annie Blaker • Last of the Tynes

The last slipway launch of a 47ft Tyne lifeboat took place at Wicklow on 28 April 2019, with Annie Blaker making a ceremonial last launch in front of hundreds of people, who had come to say farewell to the boat, which had served the Irish station for almost thirty years.

▶ Two of the Tynes sold out of service to the China Salvage & Rescue Bureau, James Burrough (ON.1093) and St Cybi II (Civil Service No.40) (ON.1094), continuing their life-saving duties in China. (By courtesy of Padstow RNLI)

to have all Tynes re-engined with new DDEC engines. By early 1997 ten boats had been converted, leaving twenty-six unconverted. The cost was £90,000 per boat, provided the work was carried our during a scheduled refit. However, the RNLI later determined that those boats with an estimated lifespan of less than nine years would not be considered for re-engining as it was deemed not to be cost effective. In the event, the programme was further curtailed, and in the end only fifteen boats were fitted with the new engines; of these, eleven had DDEC 2.5 and four had DDEC 3 engines.

There were further modifications to the boats during the early years of the twenty-first century after the RNLI developed a computer model to test self-righting ability, and applied this retrospectively to the Tyne. The simulation indicated that, in the unlikely situation that a Tyne was carrying a large number of survivors in particularly challenging sea conditions, it may possibly not self-right as designed. Therefore, it was decided to install a pair of airbags on the aft cabin roof of all Tynes. The programme began in October 2004 and was completed by May 2005, with the work being relatively straightforward as the RNLI had long experience in the use of air-bags in previous classes of lifeboats.

▼ The former Cromer lifeboat Ruby and Arthur Reed II (ON.1097), the RNLI's sixth Tyne to be built, at Shekou in China in 2013. Eight Tynes were sold to the China Salvage & Rescue Bureau, including the first six.

Tyne lifeboats to the rescue

The Tyne class lifeboats gave excellent service to the RNLI. The forty boats performed thousands of rescues, and saved many lives during their careers. Several of the Tynes were involved in outstanding rescues which were recognised by the RNLI, who awarded medals for gallantry to those Coxswains and crews involved. The following accounts describe the medal services undertaken in the Tynes.

LOWESTOFT · 19 October 1988 · Bronze medal awarded to Coxswain John Catchpole in recognition of his courage and seamanship when Spirit of Lowestoft rescued the crew of five of the coaster Medina D, which had run aground and was sinking on the south side of the Corton Channel, five miles from Lowestoft, in a strong east-south-easterly force eight gale and heavy breaking seas.

FRASERBURGH · 13 January 1989 · Thanks of the Institution on Vellum accorded to Coxswain Albert Sutherland, for the rescue of the crew of eight from the fishing vessel Mystic, which was in difficulty two

◀ Two Coxswains of Tyne lifeboats who were recipients of medals for gallantry: John Catchpole of Lowestoft (left) and Albert Sutherland of Fraserburgh. (By courtesy of the RNLI)

and a half miles from Kinnaird Head in force eight to nine winds, rough seas and an 8ft swell. The 74ft trawler lay stopped across the wind and tide, down by the head, with a severe list to port, and was rolling heavily.

ST DAVIDS • 26 February 1989 • Bronze medal awarded to Coxswain/Mechanic David Chant in recognition of the courage, seamanship and boathandling skill he displayed when Garside rescued the crew of four of the fishing vessel Stephanie Jane. The vessel had broken down and was dragging her anchor near rocks, five cables south of the South Bishop lighthouse, in a strong force eight to nine westerly gale and very rough seas, with waves estimated at 20-30ft in height. The casualty was towed to Milford Haven in extremely difficult conditions.

TEESMOUTH • 26 August 1989 • Bronze medal awarded to Coxswain Peter Race for the service to the fishing vessel Gang Warily, which had been driven aground in the dark at the foot of a sheer 360ft cliff, with 12ft seas breaking heavily and an onshore force seven wind. Redcar's Atlantic 21 Lord Brotherton was first on scene, and Redcar crew Peter Hodge swam with a line, but was washed ashore with the two survivors. The relief lifeboat Owen and Ann Aisher was taken into the surf bow first, with the engines being used to hold station as seas broke heavily over her stern. The Tyne's inflatable X-boat, manned by Christopher Jones, was launched and took the three men aboard, while the Coxswain edged the lifeboat as close as he could, with the Tyne's bow hitting submerged rocks twice. The lifeboat was eased astern through the breaking waves, and with a towline attached to the inflatable, it was successfully pulled to seaward. The inflatable was then brought alongside the lifeboat, with the four men pulled aboard and to safety at 10.13pm.

▼ Coxswain Peter Race from Teesmouth (left) and the crew involved in the service to the fishing vessel Gang Warily. (By courtesy of the RNLI)

◀ Coxswain Alan Thomas of Tenby, pictured on board the tenth Tyne RFA Sir Galahad, was awarded the Silver medal for saving the life of a fisherman trapped in his boat in September 1989. (By courtesy of the RNLI)

TENBY • 22 September 1989 • Silver medal awarded to Coxswain Alan Thomas in recognition of the outstanding courage, determination and seamanship displayed by him when RFA Sir Galahad went to the assistance of two fishing vessels in a force eight gale, poor visibility and rough seas. An attempt to tow Seeker by New Venture was being made, but this failed and Seeker ended up on the beach, with her crew being assisted ashore by the Coastguard and airlifted by helicopter. However, a third fishing vessel, Silver Stream, was struggling to keep off the beach in the north-westerly force eight to nine winds. A very large sea caught the vessel and rolled her over, filled her with water and trapped her lone skipper in the wheelhouse. Coxswain Thomas realised the man was in grave danger so manoeuvred the lifeboat into a position whereby the skipper could be pulled through the wheelhouse window by lifeboat crew on deck. The lifeboat also escorted New Venture, whose two crew were exhausted, back to Tenby Roads, where she was moored.

BALTIMORE • 30/31 October 1991 • Bronze Medal awarded to Coxswain Kieran Cotter in recognition of his determination, skill and seamanship, when the relief lifeboat Good Shepherd rescued fifteen people and saved the Spanish fishing vessel Japonica, which had suffered engine failure twenty miles west of the Fastnet Rock in storm force winds. The casualty was being driven towards the rocky shore, but the lifeboat towed the vessel, with some difficulty, to the safety of Bantry Bay. On the return passage the lifeboat put into Castletownbere to land an injured crew member and change a blocked fuel filter. While in Castletownbere, the lifeboat was called to the yacht

Coxswain Kieran Cotter (second from right) and the Baltimore lifeboat crew involved in the service to the Spanish fishing vessel Japonica using the relief lifeboat Good Shepherd, pictured in front of the station's Tyne, Hilda Jarrett, in the boathouse. (By courtesy of the RNLI)

Atlantis Adventure, which in difficulties south of the Fastnet Rock, and towed the vessel to Baltimore. The lifeboat was at sea for twenty-three hours and away from station for twenty-six hours.

SALCOMBE • 8 January 1992 • Bronze medal awarded to Coxswain/ Mechanic Frank Smith in recognition of his courage, seamanship, leadership and determination when Baltic Exchange II took the 1,200-ton coaster Janet C in tow and held her off the rocks at Start Point for three hours until a tug arrived. The coaster had suffered total power failure in south-westerly gale force winds and heavy seas. Coxswain/Mechanic Smith was officially on leave, but made himself available for this service because of the conditions and his knowledge of the Start Point area.

CROMER • 13 October 1993 • Bronze medal awarded to Coxswain Richard Davies in recognition of his courage, leadership and outstanding seamanship when Ruby and Arthur Reed II rescued the crew of five and saved the yacht Happy Bear, which had suffered steering failure off Cromer in storm force winds and 35ft seas. Heavy seas were lashing the boathouse doors as the lifeboat launched down the slipway and, on reaching the water, she was completely buried in the seas. The launch of the lifeboat was the roughest that the station had experienced in the thirty years that the coxswain had been involved.

APPLEDORE • 31 March 1994 • Bronze medal awarded to Coxswain Michael Bowden for rescuing the crew of the fishing vessel Torridge

Coxswain Richard Davies, from Cromer, was awarded a Bronze medal for a service in 1993. (Paul Russell)

Warrior. George Gibson slipped her moorings just after 11am to help the fishing vessel, which was near Bideford Bar Buoy and had one engine out of action, and made the quickest passage possible through extremely heavy seas to reach the casualty on the edge of the surf, which was the worst experienced in thirty years. The lifeboat approached Torridge Warrior and a tow line was passed at the first attempt, enabling the vessel to be pulled clear. A course was set for Ilfracombe since conditions prevented a return to Appledore. The Ilfracombe Mersey lifeboat Spirit of Derbyshire assisted in the tow, which broke at one point.

▲ Coxswain Michael Bowden from Appledore. (By courtesy of the RNLI)

LOWESTOFT · 29 August 1996 · Bronze Second-Service clasp awarded to Coxswain John Catchpole and the Thanks of the Institution on Vellum accorded to Second Coxswain/Mechanic Shane Coleman when three people were rescued from the yacht Red House Lugger, on passage from Holland with her skipper, a schoolmaster, and four teenage pupils on board, which got into difficulties thirty miles south-east of Lowestoft in rough seas, heavy swell and storm force winds. Spirit of Lowestoft and Aldeburgh's Mersey lifeboat Freddie Cooper were both involved in the long, arduous service, arriving on scene to find the ro-ro ferry Norking standing by to provide some shelter. With great difficulty, Coxswain Ian Firman put the Aldeburgh lifeboat alongside Red House Lugger and three of the crew were snatched to safety. Second Coxswain Shane Coleman was then put aboard the yacht and helped the remaining people onto Spirit of Lowestoft. Aldeburgh lifeboat was at sea from 8am to 8pm, while the Lowestoft boat returned to station after 11.30pm.

▼ Cromer lifeboat Ruby and Arthur Reed II moored at Great Yarmouth on 17 October 1993 following the medal service to the yacht Happy Bear. (Paul Russell)

▲ The 1987-built Spirit of Lowestoft (ON.1132) served at Lowestoft for more than twenty-five years, and was one of several Tynes to operate from a mooring. She launched more than 500 times on service and was involved in a number of outstanding rescues. (By courtesy of the RNLI)

FRASERBURGH • 16 February 1997 • Bronze medal awarded to Coxswain Albert Sutherland, in recognition of his outstanding seamanship and leadership when City of Edinburgh rescued six people and saved the fishing vessel Hopecrest, which was in difficulty fifty miles north-east of the lifeboat station in very rough seas and a severe gale.

ANGLE • 5 May 1997 • Bronze medal awarded to Coxswain Jeremy Richard Rees in recognition of his high standard of seamanship, courage and leadership when the lifeboat The Lady Rank rescued the crew of four and saved the motor vessel Dale Princess which was being driven onto a sheer cliff at Skomer Island by gusting gale force winds and heavy seas on 5 May 1997. A Framed Letter of Thanks signed by the Chairman of the Institution was awarded to the crew of The Lady Rank.

THANKS INSCRIBED ON VELLUM • Services involving Tyne lifeboats

Station • *Date of service* • *Recipient(s)*	
Cromer • 29.9.1988 • Richard Davies	Workington • 13.12.2000 • John Stobbart
Fraserburgh • 13.1.1989 • Albert Sutherland	Moelfre • 17.6.2002 • Rodney Pace
Teesmouth • 26.8.1989 • Christopher Jones	Lizard • 7.7.2004 • Philip Burgess
Wick • 5.3.1991 • Walter McLeod McPhee	Padstow • 25.6.2007 • Alan Tarby
Wick • 11.5.1992 • Walter McLeod McPhee	St Davids • 6.3.2008 • David John
St Helier • 17.4.1995 • Robert Vezier	Lowestoft • 13.11.2009 • John Fox
Shoreham • 2.6.1999 • Peter Huxtable	Workington • 7.12.2011 • John Stobbart and Andrew Philip Rodgers
St Davids • 24.12.1999 • Malcolm Gray	

The Tynes, boat by boat

Between 1981 and 1990 the RNLI built forty Tyne class lifeboats, primarily for service at stations where slipway launching was practised. But although the Tyne was conceived as a slipway-launched lifeboat, its hull shape and protected propellers made it ideal for operating in shallow waters. As a result, some stations where the lifeboat was kept afloat, but had to operate over sand bars or rocks, or had access problems at low tide, were also allocated Tynes. These stations included Lowestoft and Whitby on the east coast, Montrose and Portpatrick in Scotland, Arranmore and Lough Swilly in Ireland, and Salcombe, St Helier and Appledore in south-west England. Production continued until 1990, and ceased with 47-040 (ON.1158).

Replacement of the Tynes began during the 2000s, after the new 16m Tamar design had been developed. From 2006 Tamars began replacing many of Tynes, and as the Tynes ended their service they were disposed of, with a number being sold to foreign lifeboat organisations. The last Tyne to leave service was Annie Blaker (ON.1153), at Wicklow (see page 21), which was replaced in April 2019. By this time, the Tynes had given operational service with the RNLI for almost four decades in total.

NOTE The figures in brackets after each boats' dates at a station indicate the number of launches which were undertaken and the number of lives saved.

▼ Four unmarked Tynes ready to be sold out of service, at Souter Shipyard, Cowes, June 2007. (Peter Edey)

47-001 • City of London

47-001 on reexercise at Selsey.
(By courtesy of the RNLI)

OFFICIAL NUMBER 1074
BUILT 1981, Fairey Allday Marine, Cowes
YARD NO FM 708
DONOR City of London Appeal
COST £433,485
NAMED 1.11.1982 at Fishmongers Hall Steps, London Bridge, by the Lady Mayoress of London, Lady Leaver; rededicated 26.5.1984 at Selsey

STATIONS
Selsey 2.11.1983 – 2.2006 (415/58)
DISPOSAL Sold 2007 to China Salvage & Rescue Bureau, shipped to China 11.7.2007, took one month to reach Hong Kong, and stationed at Xiamen (Amoy) Base, Donghai Bureau
RENAMED Huaying 388

▲ 47-001 being launched for lifeboat day at Selsey in August 1991. (Nicholas Leach)

▲ 47-001 off Selsey after her last launch, prior to her withdrawal from service, February 2006. (John Periam)

47-002 • Sam and Joan Woods

47-002 on relief duty at Appledore.

OFFICIAL NUMBER 1075
BUILT 1982, Fairey Allday Marine, Cowes
YARD NO FM 709
DONOR RNLI General Funds
COST £432,628
NAMED 28.6.1984 at RNLI Depot, Poole, by Mrs A.W. Hemsted, daughter of Admiral Sir Wilfred Woods, former Chairman of RNLI Committee of Management

STATIONS
Relief 1984 – 1993 (59/24)
Walton and Frinton 1.8.1993 – 5.1996 (67/10)
Relief 5.1996 – 2006 (94/9)
DISPOSAL Sold 2007 to China Salvage & Rescue Bureau, taken from Felixstowe by container ship in July 2007, stationed at Ningbo Base, Donghai Bureau
RENAMED Huaying 389

▲ 47-002 heading out of Lowestoft while on relief duty in Suffolk, September 2003. (Peter Edey)

▲ 47-002 at Buckie Shipyard, April 2006, just before she was withdrawn from service. (Nicholas Leach)

47-003 • James Burrough

47-003 afloat for lifeboat day at Padstow.

OFFICIAL NUMBER 1094
BUILT 1984, Fairey Allday Marine, Cowes
YARD NO FM 716
DONOR Gift of Miss H.B. 'Mickie' Allen, East Clandon, Guildford, Surrey, in memory of her great-grandfather and as a tribute to lifeboat crews
COST £451,906.01
NAMED 15.4.1985 at the North Quay, Padstow, by Miss H.B. Allen

STATIONS
Padstow 28.12.1984 – 17.7.2006 (293/97)
Relief 7.2006 – 2007 (12/0)
DISPOSAL Sold 2007 to China Salvage & Rescue Bureau, shipped to China 8.8.2007, stationed at Yantai Base, Beihai Bureau and later Rongcheng Base
RENAMED Huaying 386

▲ 47-003 on exercise with RNAS Sea King helicopter in the Camel Estuary. (Paul Richards)

▲ 47-003 out of the water, having been given the RNLI's modern livery. (Peter Edey)

47-004 • St Cybi II (Civil Service No.40)

47-004 on service at Holyhead.

OFFICIAL NUMBER 1095

BUILT 1985, Fairey Marine hull, William Osborne fit out, Cowes/Littlehampton

YARD NO FM 717

DONOR The Civil Service, Post Office and British Telecom Lifeboat Fund

COST £449,412.90

NAMED 26.4.1986 by Lady Armstrong, wife of Robert Armstrong, Head of the Civil Service

STATIONS

Holyhead 20.9.1985 – 12.1997 (267/119)

Relief 12.1997 – 2006 (106/5)

DISPOSAL Sold 2007 to China Salvage & Rescue Bureau; shipped to China 8.8.2007, stationed at Rongcheng Base, Beihai Bureau; later moved to Tianjin Base, Beihai Bureau

RENAMED Huaying 387

▲ 47-004 returning to Holyhead after a routine publicity trip in June 1990. (Nicholas Leach)

▲ 47-004 on the slipway at Douglas, Isle of Man, while on relief duty, July 2005. (Nicholas Leach)

47-005 • Ethel Anne Measures

47-005 on exercise off Mumbles.

OFFICIAL NUMBER 1096
BUILT 1985, Fairey Allday Marine, Cowes
YARD NO FM 718
DONOR The James Frederick and Ethel Anne Measures Charity, Mumbles Lifeboat Appeal, the Lord Mayor of Birmingham Appeal and Pebble Mill Appeal
COST £447,453.14
NAMED 3.7.1985 at Swansea Marina by HRH Duke of Kent, President of the RNLI

STATIONS
Mumbles 31.7.1985 – 7.2006 (364/70)
Relief 2006 – 3.2007 (3/0)
DISPOSAL Sold 2007 to China Salvage & Rescue Bureau, shipped to China via Felixstowe, served at Beihai Bureau, and in 2012 became a lifeboat at Rongcheng stations, Nanhai Bureau
RENAMED Huaying 384

▲ 47-005 being launched from the lifeboat house at Mumbles, April 1998. (Nicholas Leach)

▲ 47-005 prior to being recovered into the lifeboat house at Mumbles, July 2003. (Nicholas Leach)

47-006 • Ruby and Arthur Reed II

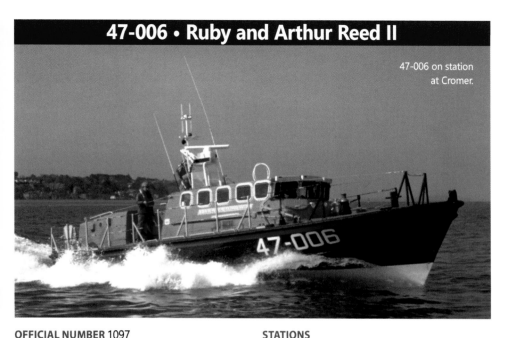

47-006 on station at Cromer.

OFFICIAL NUMBER 1097

BUILT 1985, Fairey Allday Marine, Cowes

YARD NO FM 719

DONOR Bequest of Mrs R.M. Reed, with special local appeal, gifts and legacies

COST £439,560.95

NAMED 20.6.1986 at Cromer by HRH Duke of Kent

STATIONS

Cromer 16.12.1985 – 11.1996 (75/29)

Relief 1996 – 1999 (28/0)

Cromer 24.3.1999 – 2007 (45/9)

DISPOSAL Sold 7.2008 to China Salvage & Rescue Bureau; shipped to China in 9.2007 for service at Haikou stations, Nanhai Bureau.

RENAMED Huaying 385

▲ 47-0006 on exercise off Cromer pier, May 2006. (Nicholas Leach)

▲ 47-006 at Goodchild Marine, Burgh Castle, after refit, February 2002. (Peter Edey)

The 47ft Tyne class lifeboat

MAIN PHOTO Sarah Emily Harrop and Alexander Coutanche passing Calshot lifeboat's mooring buoy and boarding boat, with Hamble River entrance in the background left and Hook Buoy on the extreme right, marking the main channel to the Port of Southampton, January 2010. (Nicholas Leach)

47-007 • City of Edinburgh

47-007 on station at Fraserburgh.

OFFICIAL NUMBER 1109

BUILT 1985, Fairey Allday Marine, Cowes

YARD NO FM 1058

DONOR The City of Edinburgh Lifeboat Appeal

COST £454,597

NAMED 25.6.1986 at Fraserburgh by HRH Duke of Kent

STATIONS

Fraserburgh 3.11.1985 – 8.5.2002 (180/115)

Relief 5.2002 – 2008 (61/0)

DISPOSAL Sold 2010 to ADES, Uruguay, for use as a lifeboat; shipped to South America in 2011 for use by ADES at Puerto de Colonia

RENAMED ADES 19 Centenario BSE

▲ 47-007 on relief duty at Montrose, setting out on exercise, August 2002. (Nicholas Leach)

▲ 47-007 as a lifeboat in Uruguay having been renamed ADES 19 Centenario BSE.

47-008 • Phil Mead

47-008 on exercise
at Teesmouth.

OFFICIAL NUMBER 1110
BUILT 1986, Fairey Allday Marine, Cowes
YARD NO FM 1059
DONOR Trustees of the Phil Mead Charitable
Trust, and local appeal
COST £459,511.53
NAMED 14.9.1986 at Tees Dock, Grangetown, by
Mrs Muriel Mead in memory of her late husband

STATIONS
Teesmouth 23.1.1986 – 29.4.2006 (346/42)
Relief 2006 – 2008 (10/3)
DISPOSAL Sold 6.2008 to China Rescue &
Salvage Bureau, for service as a lifeboat at
Shenzhen stations, Nanhai Bureau
RENAMED Huaying 382

▲ 47-008 in the Tees estuary during Teesmouth's
annual lifeboat day, July 1994. (Nicholas Leach)

▲ 47-008 at the RNLI Depot, Poole, in February 2007
prior to being sold. (Nicholas Leach)

47-009 • William Luckin

47-009 on exercise off Arranmore. (Rick Tomlinson, by courtesy of the RNLI)

OFFICIAL NUMBER 1111

BUILT 1986, Fairey Allday Marine, Cowes

YARD NO FM 1060

DONOR Bequest of Mrs Rose Mary Luckin

COST £456,592.12

NAMED 30.8.1986 at Arranmore by Mrs Penelope Kavanagh, chair of RNLI Dublin

STATIONS

Arranmore 5.4.1986 – 1.2000 (280/46)

Lough Swilly 4.2001 – 6.2007 (67/8)

DISPOSAL Sold 6.2008 to China Rescue & Salvage Bureau, shipped out in 7.2008 for service as a rescue boat at Guangzhou stations in the Nanhai Bureau

RENAMED Huaying 383

▲ 47-009 during the early years of her career stationed at Arranmore. (By courtesy of the RNLI)

▲ 47-009 on exercise at Lough Swilly in April 2002, where she served for six years. (Nicholas Leach)

47-010 • RFA Sir Galahad

47-010 on relief duty at Bembridge.

OFFICIAL NUMBER 1112

BUILT 1986, Wright, Derby/William Osborne, Littlehampton

YARD NO WO 2880

DONOR Special appeal by the Royal Fleet Auxiliary, together with other appeals, gifts and legacies

COST £450,000

NAMED 29.9.1986 by HRH Princess Alexandra at the Pier, Tenby

STATIONS

Tenby 6.9.1986 – 4.2006 (365/74)

Relief 4.2006 – 2.2008 (29/0)

Angle 26.2.2008 – 3.2009 (20/0)

DISPOSAL Sold 1.2010 to Geoffrey Williams, based in the dock at Port Penrhyn, near Bangor, largely unaltered; she was the first Tyne to be sold out of service to a private individual; sold in May 2022 to new a owner and taken to Lochinver

RENAMED Sir Galahad

▲ 47-010 being launched at Tenby during her early service career. (By courtesy of the RNLI)

▲ 47-010 moored at Lochinver, Highland, Scotland, February 2023. (Iain McPherson)

47-011 • The Lady Rank

47-011 on exercise off Angle.

OFFICIAL NUMBER 1114
BUILT 1987, Wright, Derby/William Osborne, Littlehampton
YARD NO WO 2970
DONOR The Rank Foundation
NAMED 6.8.1987 at Angle Pier by the Hon Mrs Shelagh Cowen
COST £535,803.60

STATIONS
Angle 23.6.1987 – 26.2.2008 (271/29)
Relief 26.2.2008 – 2011 (26/0)
DISPOSAL Sold 7.2011 to ADES, the Uruguayan lifeboat service, and shipped to Uruguay from Devonport
RENAMED ADES 20 Bicentenary BSE

▲ 47-011 out of the water at the RNLI, Depot, Poole in April 2005. (Nicholas Leach)

▲ 47-011 renamed ADES 20 Bicentenary BSE in service with the Uruguayan lifeboat service.

47-012 on relief duty at
Fleetwood, February 1997.

OFFICIAL NUMBER 1115

BUILT 1987, Wright, Derby/William Osborne

YARD NO WO 2990

DONOR The Church Appeal

COST £543,916.89

NAMED 14.4.1988 at St Katharine Docks, London,
by the Most Rev and Rt Hon Robert Runcie, MC,
DD, Lord Archbishop of Canterbury

STATIONS

Relief 1988 – 2010 (239/74)

DISPOSAL Sold 6.2010 to Inverness Harbour
Trust, used as a pilot boat at Inverness and based
in Inverness Marina, remaining largely unaltered
apart from adaptations for pilotage work

RENAMED Carnarc

▲ 47-012 out of the water at the RNLI Depot, Poole,
May 2006. (Nicholas Leach)

▲ 47-012 renamed Carnarc and berthed at Inverness
Marina, May 2012. (Nicholas Leach)

47-013 • Robert and Violet

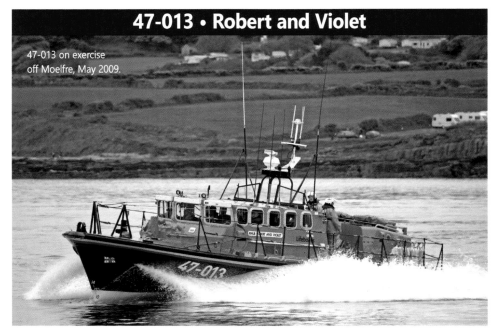

47-013 on exercise off Moelfre, May 2009.

OFFICIAL NUMBER 1116
BUILT 1987, hull by Wright, Derby; fit out by Lochin Marine, Rye
YARD NO WO 11160
DONOR Anonymous gift
COST £532,057
NAMED 2.7.1988 by Mrs Lesley Roberts, wife of Moelfre Coxswain William Roberts

STATIONS
Moelfre 22.1.1988 – 5.2013 (394/92)
Lough Swilly 26.5.2013 – 4.2015 (16/0)
DISPOSAL Sold 7.2015 to Master Divers, Sri Lanka for use by the Sri Lankan Lifeboat Institution, transported to Sri Lanka on a container ship from Felixstowe
RENAMED Puffin XII

▲ 47-013 returning to Moelfre in 1995, with, unusually, the operational number in yellow. (Nicholas Leach)

▲ 47-013 after being sold by the RNLI, arriving in Sri Lanka and being lifted ashore, July 2015.

47-014 • James Bibby

47-014 on relief at Lough Swilly, April 2009.

OFFICIAL NUMBER 1117
BUILT 1986, Fairey Allday Marine, Cowes
YARD NO FM 1073
DONOR The gift from John Benjamin Bibby, Liverpool, in memory of his grandfather
COST £528,430
NAMED 16.5.1987 at British Nuclear Fuels Ltd, Ramsden Dock, Barrow by Miss Lindsay Bibby, daughter of the donor

STATIONS
Barrow 4.9.1986 – 1.2008 (202/14)
Relief 1.2008 – 2010 (39/0)
DISPOSAL Sold 2.2011 to Macdonald Ferries, Invergordon, for use as a ferry and workboat, with the aft cabin removed; out of the water at Nigg for many years, bought in 2023 by Ian Fraser, and taken to Clydebank
RENAMED Pioneer

▲ 47-014 putting out from Barrow on exercise, April 1996. (Nicholas Leach)

▲ 47-014 renamed Pioneer out of the water at Nigg, near Cromarty, 2022. (Nicholas Leach)

47-015 • Hetty Rampton

47-015 on exercise off Porthdinllaen.

OFFICIAL NUMBER 1120
BUILT 1987, Fairey Allday Marine, Cowes
YARD NO FM 1106
DONOR Trustees of Miss Hetty Mabel Rampton's Charitable Settlement
COST £508,696.17
NAMED 18.8.1987 at Porthdinllaen by Miss Yolande Rampton, niece of the donor

STATIONS
Porthdinllaen 27.4.1987 – 8.2012 (316/52)
Relief 24.8.2012 – 2015 (3/0)
DISPOSAL Sold 2015 to Montrose Port Authority, for use as a pilot boat based in Montrose; delivered to new owner in February 2016
RENAMED Inch Burn

▲ 47-015 launching on exercise down the slipway at Porthdinllaen, April 1996. (Nicholas Leach)

▲ 47-015 at Montrose, renamed Inch Burn and in use as a pilot boat, July 2021. (Nicholas Leach)

47-016 • Norman Salvesen

47-016 on station at Sennen Cove.

OFFICIAL NUMBER 1121
BUILT 1988, Wright, Derby/Harrison, Amble
YARD NO 1121
ENGINES Twin 425hp General Motors 6V-92-TA/ 1997- 565hp General Motors 6V-92TA DDEC
DONOR Bequest of Mrs Mary 'Mickie' Salvesen
NAMED 16.9.1988 at the North Pier, Wick, by Mrs Bright Gordon, MBE, after donor's husband

STATIONS Wick 16.9.1988 – 2.1997 (120/54), Sennen Cove 5.12.1998 – 10.2009 (130/10), Relief 10.2009 – 2014 (10/0)
DISPOSAL Sold 6.2014 to Captain William 'Ben' Roberts, taken to North Wales and kept in Conwy Marina as a pleasure boat, retaining her lifeboat appearance externally
RENAMED Norman Salvesen

▲ 47-016 berthed in Wick harbour, July 1995; she was initially slipway launched at Wick. (Nicholas Leach)

▲ 47-016 berthed in Conwy Marina, March 2017, under private ownership. (Nicholas Leach)

47-017 • Owen and Ann Aisher

47-017 served in the relief fleet for her entire career. (By courtesy of the RNLI)

OFFICIAL NUMBER 1122
BUILT 1988, Wright, Derby/W.A. Souter, Cowes
YARD NO WO 0012
DONOR Gift of Sir Owen Aisher, well known yachtsman, Chairman of Marley Tile Company
NAMED 18.8.1988 at RNLI Depot, Poole, by Lady Ann Aisher
STATIONS Relief 1988 – 2012 (315/66)

DISPOSAL Sold 6.2013 to the Richardson Brothers Foundation and used by the MVS and a Sea Scout organisation on the Thames. After being damaged at a boatyard, she was sold in 6.2017 to Montrose Harbour Authority, who bought the boat for use as spares for the two other Tynes they operated as pilot boats.
RENAMED MVS Prince George V 104

▲ 47-017 on relief duty at Kilmore Quay, July 2005. (Nicholas Leach)

▲ 47-017 renamed Prince George on the River Thames, May 2014. (Peter Edey)

47-018 • Max Aitken III

47-018 on exercise off Bembridge.

OFFICIAL NUMBER 1126
BUILT 1987, Fairey Allday Marine, Cowes
YARD NO FM 1189
DONOR The Beaverbrook Foundation.
NAMED 10.9.1987 at North Quay, Bembridge Harbour by Lady Beaverbrook
STATIONS
Bembridge 24.8.1987 – 5.2.2009 (479/141)
Relief 2.2009 – 5.2012 (30/1)
DISPOSAL Sold 31.5.2013 to Rea Associates

Ltd, Rowlands Castle, Hampshire, resold from Portchester and taken by road to Goodchild Marine, Burgh Castle for survey, and in May 2017 was offered for sale again. In 2018 she was acquired by Jersey Lifeboat Association, left Burgh Castle on 11.6.2018 and sailed to St Helier, Jersey, arriving on 13.6.2018, where she was prepared for service; she became a declared rescue facility on 11.4.2019 at St Helier.
RENAMED Sir Max Aitken III

▲ 47-018 on exercise off Bembridge, July 1996, in her original livery. (Nicholas Leach)

▲ 47-018 at St Helier, renamed Sir Max Aitken III, operated by Jersey Lifeboat Association. (Ian Moignard)

47-019 • Babs and Agnes Robertson

47-019 on exercise off Mumbles.

OFFICIAL NUMBER 1127
BUILT 1987, Fairey Allday Marine, Cowes
YARD NO FM 1190
DONOR Gift from The Robertson Trust, founded by the Misses Robertson of Robertson and Baxter Ltd, Scotch Whisky Blenders, Glasgow
COST £535,421.53
NAMED 21.5.1988 at Peterhead by Mrs Bruce McNeil after two sisters

STATIONS
Peterhead 14.1.1988 – 4.2006 (215/33)
Relief 29.4.2006 – 7.2006 (3/0)
Mumbles 15.7.2006 – 10.2.2014 (129/0)
DISPOSAL Sold 2014 to Barry Johnston, Orkney, for use as a trip boat and for crew transfers in the renewables industry for Fast Vessel Charters, based in Stromness; sold in 2017 and taken by road to Portishead Marina in July 2017
RENAMED FVC 1

▲ 47-019 berthed in Peterhead harbour, August 1998, ten years after she arrived on station. (Nicholas Leach)

▲ 47-019 renamed FVC1 at Portishead Quays Marina, November 2022. (Nicholas Leach)

47-020 • Spirit of Lowestoft

47-020 on exercise off Lowestoft.

OFFICIAL NUMBER 1132
BUILT 1987, Fairey Allday Marine, Cowes
YARD NO FM 1191
DONOR The Lowestoft Lifeboat Appeal, together with the bequest of Albert Frederick Worboys and other gifts and legacies
COST £520,166
NAMED 26.5.1988 at Lowestoft by HRH Duke of Kent

STATIONS
Lowestoft 16.11.1987 – 2.10.2014 (560/83)
Relief 2.10.2014 – 2018 (0/0)
DISPOSAL Placed on display as part of the Historic Lifeboat Collection, Chatham Historic Dockyard; she arrived at Chatham on 18.6.2019 to be exhibited in the covered slipway
RENAMED Spirit of Lowestoft

▲ 47-020 departing Lowestoft harbour on exercise, March 1995. (Nicholas Leach)

▲ 47-020 on display as part of the Lifeboat Collection at the Historic Dockyard Chatham. (Nicholas Leach)

47-021 • The Famous Grouse

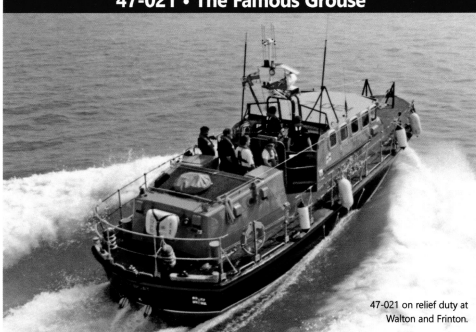

47-021 on relief duty at
Walton and Frinton.

OFFICIAL NUMBER 1133
BUILT 1987, Fairey Allday Marine, Cowes
YARD NO FM 1192
DONOR The Famous Grouse Competition Appeal
COST £531,587.71
NAMED 11.12.1987 at Cowes by Mrs C.M. Barrie,
of the Old Mill Hotel, Motherwell

STATIONS
Relief 12.12.1987 – 4.2004 (174/37)
Kilmore Quay 7.4.2004 – 10.2010 (187/0)
Relief 27.10.2010 – 2012 (0/0)
DISPOSAL Sold 2013 to Canadian Lifeboat
Institution, used as a lifeboat at Steveston
RENAMED Fraser Lifeboat 1A-04

▲ 47-021 berthed in the marina at Kilmore Quay,
April 2007. (Nicholas Leach)

▲ 47-021 in Canada as Fraser Lifeboat 1A-04; she is
based at Steveston, which is on the Fraser River.

47-022 heading into
Salcombe harbour.

OFFICIAL NUMBER 1130
BUILT 1988, Wright, Derby/Lochin Marine, Rye
YARD NO 1130
DONOR The Baltic Exchange with other gifts and
legacies
COST £584,362
NAMED 12.6.1989 at Salcombe by Mr David
Frame, Chairman of the Baltic Exchange

STATIONS
Salcombe 30.8.1988 – 10.3.2008 (478/135)
Relief 3.2008 – 2009 (23/0)
DISPOSAL Sold 2010 to Seychelles via the
Foreign & Commonwealth Office, used on anti-
piracy patrols and fisheries enforcement duties
of the Seychelles inner islands and northern
approaches, operated by the Seychelles Coast
Guard from its base on the island of Mahé
RENAMED PB Fortune

▲ 47-022 at the RNLI Depot, Poole, April 2007.

▲ 47-022 ready for shipping to the Seychelles.

47-023 • City of Sheffield

47-023 on station at Poole, February 2016.
(Andy Lyons, by courtesy of the RNLI)

OFFICIAL NUMBER 1131
BUILT 1988, Wright, Derby/W.A. Souter, Cowes
YARD NO 0027
DONOR The City of Sheffield Lifeboat Appeal,
with the bequest of Mrs Mary Mabel Walker and
other gifts and legacies
COST £587,664.13
NAMED 28.7.1989 at Whitby by HRH The
Duchess of Kent

STATIONS
Whitby 12.12.1988 – 4.1996 (239/88)
Ramsgate 17.4.1996 – 27.9.1996 (18/6)
Hartlepool 24.7.1997 – 10.2000 (31/8)
Relief 10.2000 – 9.2001 (7/0)
Poole 5.9.2001 – 12.11.2016 (554/1)
DISPOSAL Sold 6.2017, displayed at the National
Emergency Services Museum in Sheffield; moved
from Poole by road 6.2017
RENAMED City of Sheffield

▲ 47-023 on station at Hartlepool, the third station
she service, May 1999. (Nicholas Leach)

▲ 47-023 on display at the National Emergency
Services Museum, Sheffield, June 2017. (Martin Fish)

47-024 • Hilda Jarrett

47-024 on exercise at Baltimore, April 2010.

OFFICIAL NUMBER 1137
BUILT 1987, Fairey Allday Marine, Cowes
YARD NO FM 1193
DONOR Bequest of Mrs Hilda Jesse Jarrett, together with RNLI funds
COST £544,871
NAMED 17.9.1988 at Baltimore by Mrs Elizabeth Love, wife of Clayton Love jnr, Chairman of the RNLI' Ireland Committee
STATIONS
Baltimore 3.3.1988 – 3.2012 (360/92)

Relief 3.2012 – 7.2015 (10/0)
DISPOSAL Sold 7.7.2015 to Montrose Port Authority to and converted into a pilot boat by Mackay Builders, Arbroath; she was formally renamed on 25.9.2015 at Montrose; the naming ceremony was carried out by Justine Scott-Gray, wife of Nik Scott-Gray, chief executive of the Port Authority; she was replaced as a pilot boat in December 2022 and sold, being taken to the west coast of Scotland in March 2023
RENAMED North Esk

▲ 47-024 on exercise off the coast of County Cork in her original livery. (By courtesy of the RNLI)

▲ 47-024 as the well maintained pilot boat North Esk at Montrose, July 2021. (Nicholas Leach)

47-025 • Lord Saltoun

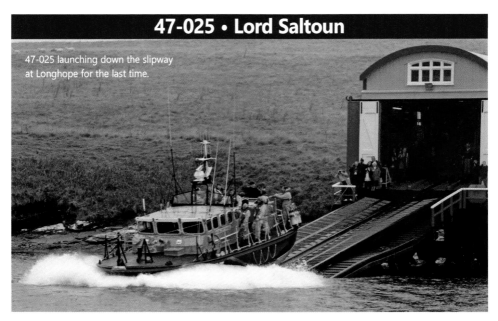

47-025 launching down the slipway at Longhope for the last time.

OFFICIAL NUMBER 1138
BUILT 1988, Fairey Allday Marine, Cowes
YARD NO FM 1194
DONOR Bequest of Mrs Mary Salvesen
COST £539,488
NAMED 22.7.1988 at Longhope pier by Lady Saltoun, daughter of the late Lord Saltoun

STATIONS
Longhope 10.3.1988 – 8.1999 (41/9)
Relief 8.1999 – 2.2012 (111/6)
DISPOSAL Sold 2012 to David Ferran and Sons Ltd, Belfast, and used to take ships' crews out to their vessel, stores and survey work, and as a relief pilot boat at Belfast; in 2018 was out of the water at Carrickfergus, for sale
RENAMED Norma-G

▲ 47-025 in between relief duties, moored at Whitehaven, January 2012. (Nicholas Leach)

▲ 47-025 renamed Norma-G out of the water at Carrickfergus, July 2021. (Nicholas Leach)

47-026 • Garside

47-026 departing
St Davids in 2016.

OFFICIAL NUMBER 1139
BUILT 1988, Fairey Allday Marine, Cowes
YARD NO FM 1195
DONOR Bequests of Thomas Harold Garside and his sister, Miss Dorothy Garside
COST £557,151
NAMED 2.6.1989 at St Justinian, St Davids by HRH The Duke of Kent

STATIONS
St Davids 25.5.1988 – 21.10.2016 (345/79)
DISPOSAL Sold 2018 to Falmouth Docks and Engineering Company, where she was used as a port work boat at Falmouth Docks
RENAMED Triton

▲ 47-026 being recovered up the slipway at St Davids after a service launch, August 2008. (Nicholas Leach)

▲ 47-026 berthed at Falmouth Docks in service with the Port Authority, August 2021. (EFAS)

47-027 • George Gibson

47-027 at Appledore in her original livery. (By courtesy of the RNLI)

OFFICIAL NUMBER 1140
BUILT 1988, Fairey Allday Marine, Cowes
YARD NO FM 1196
DONOR Mr George C. Gibson OBE, through the Gibson Charitable Trust
COST £551,725.63
NAMED 25.6.1988 by Mrs Frank Homfray, daughter of donor, at Appledore
STATIONS
Appledore 19.6.1988 – 3.2010 (259/22)

Relief 3.2010 – 2011 (13/0)
DISPOSAL Sold 2013, via a broker, to Specialist Group International, to be used as a construction safety vessel on the North Somerset Coast for the new Hinkley Point Power Station, with the hull resprayed orange at Berthon Boat Co, Lymington, to match the upperworks, and has been at Watchet and Portishead Marina
RENAMED The John Faulding

▲ 47-027 heading out of the Torridge estuary on exercise at Appledore, July 2007. (Nicholas Leach)

▲ 47-027 renamed The John Faulding, out of the water at Portishead, August 2020. (Nicholas Leach)

47-028 • Sir John Fisher

47-028 on exercise at Workington.

OFFICIAL NUMBER 1141
BUILT 1989, Wright hull, Marshall-Branson fit out, Derby/Amble
YARD NO FM 1141
DONOR The Sir John Fisher Foundation; bequests of Frances Elizabeth Jackson and Mabel Annie Young; together with other gifts and RNLI general funds
COST £628,308

NAMED 24.4.1993 at Workington by Mrs Diane Meacock, trustee of the Sir John Fisher Foundation
STATIONS
Relief 1989 – 6.1992 (5/0)
Workington 8.6.1992 – 4.2017 (270/50)
DISPOSAL Sold 2018, taken from Poole to Whitehaven, then to a boatyard at Clydebank, before moving to Troon Marina in 2021
RENAMED Eala

▲ 47-028 being recovered by the unique davit launch system at Workington, October 2016. (Nicholas Leach)

▲ 47-028 renamed Eala at Troon Marina, Ayrshire, May 2022. (Nicholas Leach)

47-029 • Mariners Friend

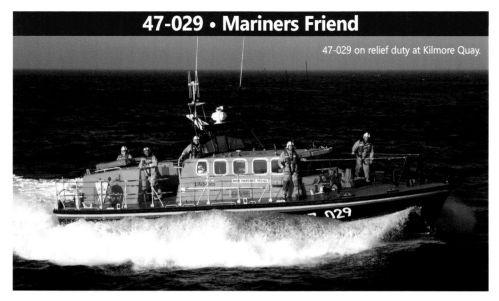

47-029 on relief duty at Kilmore Quay.

OFFICIAL NUMBER 1142
BUILT 1989, Wright, Derby/W. A. Souter, Cowes
YARD NO 0056
DONOR The H. B. Allen Charitable Trust.
COST £615,808
NAMED 20.9.1989 at RNLI's Cowes Depot, Isle of Wight, by donor Miss H.B. 'Mickie' Allen
STATIONS
Relief 12.1989 – 6.2007 (190/49)
Lough Swilly 24.6.2007 – 10.2012 (46/1)

Relief 10.2012 – 1.2013 (0/0)
DISPOSAL Sold 5.2014 to Andrew Holman, owner of Kilfinchen Estate, Isle of Mull; painted blue at Hamble, then transported by road to Glasgow, and sailed via the Crinan Canal to the Isle of Mull, where she was used as a work boat on Loch Scridain; she was converted at Dunstaffnage Marina, Oban, and winters there.
RENAMED Suilbhir Giomach (Jolly Lobster)

▲ 47-029 on relief duty at Lowestoft, June 1994, in her original livery. (Nicholas Leach)

▲ 47-029 out of the water at Dunstaffnage, February 2018. (Cliff Crone)

47-030 • David Robinson

47-030 Launching on exercise at Lizard.

OFFICIAL NUMBER 1145
BUILT 1988, Fairey Allday Marine, Cowes
YARD NO FM 1208
DONOR Legacy of the late Sir David Robinson
COST £550,132
NAMED 13.5.1989 at the Lizard by Mrs Jean
Baker, daughter of donor
STATIONS
Lizard 17.8.1988 – 16.7.2011 (211/89)
Relief 7.2011 – 2016 (16/0)

DISPOSAL Sold 7.4.2017 to Togo Oil and Marine
for crew transfer work at the anchorage, Lome,
Togo, West Africa; taken to Holyhead for refit,
painting, removal of the aft accommodation and
installation of a hatch, air conditioning and heavy
rubber fendering; taken to Conwy by road, to the
South Coast and then to Togo.
RENAMED Diligence

▲ 47-030 on exercise at off Kilcobben Cove, the
Lizard, April 2010. (Nicholas Leach)

▲ 47-030 at Conwy Marina having had her aft cabin
removed, September 2017. (Nicholas Leach)

47-031 • Voluntary Worker

47-031 at Lytham St Annes.

OFFICIAL NUMBER 1146
BUILT 1988, Fairey Allday Marine, Cowes
YARD NO FM 1209
DONOR Volvo Concessionaries Ltd, Tesco Stores Ltd Promotions, and other gifts; named in recognition of the work of crews, guilds, officials; gift of Mr and Mrs Frank Atkinson paid for the engines
COST £556,402
NAMED 23.9.1988 at RNLI Depot, Poole, by Mrs Jessie Brown, Honorary Secretary of Portaferry Ladies Guild; one of two lifeboats partially funded by Volvo Concessionaires
STATIONS
Lytham St Annes 1.12.1988 – 1.1990 (10/8)
Relief 20.1.1990 – 2005 (181/41)
Selsey 26.2.2006 – 10.7.2017 (197/7)
DISPOSAL Sold 2018 to Helical Technology Limited, Lytham, taken to Glasson Marina, and later brought south to Lytham.
RENAMED Voluntary Worker

▲ 47-031 being recovered at Selsey, she she served for more than ten years, July 2009. (Nicholas Leach)

▲ 47-031 moored at Lytham, retaining her lifeboat name, August 2020. (Martin Fish)

47-032 • Sir William Hillary

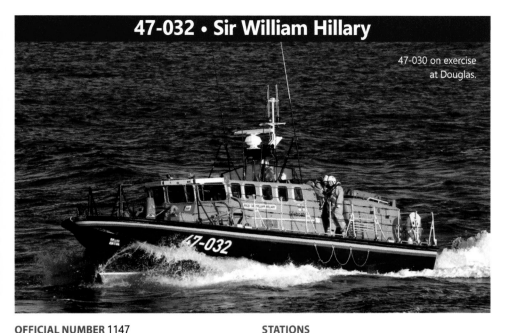

47-030 on exercise at Douglas.

OFFICIAL NUMBER 1147
BUILT 1988, Fairey Allday Marine, Cowes
YARD NO FM 1210
DONOR Legacy of the late Alan James Woolfenden, Gawsworth, Cheshire; donation from Geoffrey W. Sargeant and other gifts
COST £565,956
NAMED 21.7.1989 at Douglas by His Grace The Duke of Atholl

STATIONS
Douglas 25.11.1988 – 2.7.2018 (336/88)
DISPOSAL Sold July 2020, taken from the RNLI All-weather Lifeboat Centre at Poole to Portishead Marina, via Salcombe, Padstow and Clovelly, escorted by Mary Irene Millar.
RENAMED Sir William

▲ 47-032 outside the boathouse at the head of the slipway at Douglas. (By courtesy of the RNLI)

▲ 47-032 in Portishead Marina, renamed Sir William, August 2020. (Nicholas Leach)

47-033 on exercise
at Portpatrick.

OFFICIAL NUMBER 1151
BUILT 1989, FBM Ltd, Cowes
YARD NO 1237
DONOR Legacies of the late Mrs Mary Irene
Millar, Miss Mary Milne Stewart and Mrs Muriel
Johns in memory of her husband Captain
Bertram Johns, together with other gifts
COST £582,557.13
NAMED 19.5.1989 at Portpatrick by
Princess Alexandra

STATIONS
Portpatrick 16.3.1989 – 13.11.2011 (251/70)
Relief 13.11.2011 – 2013 (0/0)
DISPOSAL Sold 12.2013 to Keith Berry, and
initially based at Portishead Marina, remaining
unaltered; extensively toured England's south
coast, attending RNLI ceremonies and ex lifeboat
gatherings, and other maritime events; based at
Mayflower Marina, Plymouth from 2021
RENAMED Mary Irene Millar

▲ 47-033 on station at Portpatrick, moored in the
harbour, September 2002. (Nicholas Leach)

▲ 47-033 at Weymouth, July 2019, taking part in that
station's 150th anniversary parade. (Nicholas Leach)

47-034 • Moonbeam

47-034 on exercise at Montrose, April 2013.

OFFICIAL NUMBER 1152
BUILT 1989, FBM Ltd, Cowes
YARD NO 1238
DONOR Gift of Mr and Mrs Roland Sutton, of Grampian
COST £580,150.56
NAMED 1.7.1989 at Montrose by Mrs Lillian Sutton, of Collieston, Aberdeenshire

STATIONS
Montrose 28.5.1989 – 9.2015 (170/7)
DISPOSAL Sold 2016 to David Medri and kept at Portishead Marina, used as a private pleasure boat, remaining unaltered externally; participated, with 47-033, in the flotilla to mark the 40th anniversary of the Penlee lifeboat disaster; based in Salcombe from 2019
RENAMED Moonbeam

▲ 47-034 on station at Montrose, arriving at Arbroath while on exercise, August 2000. (Nicholas Leach)

▲ 47-034 at Newlyn, August 2021, for the event to mark the 40th anniversary of the Penlee lifeboat disaster.

47-035 • Annie Blaker

47-035 on exercise at Wicklow, September 2014.

OFFICIAL NUMBER 1153
BUILT 1989, FBM Ltd, Cowes
YARD NO 1239
DONOR Bequest of Annie Lydia Blaker, and RNLI general funds
COST £575,636.26
NAMED 19.5.1990 at Wicklow by Dr Patrick Hillery, President of the Republic of Ireland

STATIONS
Wicklow 8.10.1989 – 4.2019 (375/28)
DISPOSAL Sold 2019 to Jonathan Young, used as pleasure boat, based at Portishead Quays Marina; solg in February 2023 to Buz White, St Peter Port, and taken to Guernsey for use as a charter boat round the Channel Islands
RENAMED Annie Blaker

▲ 47-035 on the slipway at Wicklow, dressed overall, May 2017. (Nicholas Leach)

▲ 47-035 at St Peter Port, Guernsey. just after arriving in the Channel Islands, February 2023. (Tony Rive)

47-036 • Kenneth Thelwall II

47-036 on exercise at Walton and Frinton, June 2009.

OFFICIAL NUMBER 1154
BUILT 1989, Wright, Derby/W.A. Souter, Cowes
YARD NO 0068
DONOR Bequest of Kenneth Thelwall, Walkington, Yorkshire
COST £615,082.81
NAMED 25.10.1990 at East Pier Yard, Royal Harbour, Ramsgate by Mrs Lucia Hobson

STATIONS
Ramsgate 27.4.1990 – 29.8.1995 (116/21)
Walton and Frinton 15.5.1996 – 9.5.2011 (288/15)
DISPOSAL Sold 9.2011 to Bere Island Ferries, Co Cork, Ireland; used as a pilot and work boat by Blue Ocean Marine Ltd, Bere Island, Co Cork, little altered, operated out of Bere Island and Dingle Harbour
RENAMED Ocean Lad

▲ 47-036 entering Ramsgate harbour after her naming ceremony, 25.9.1990. (Nicholas Leach)

▲ 47-036 at Bere Island, renamed Ocean Lad, February 2012. (Nicholas Leach)

47-037 • Sarah Emily Harrop

47-037 naming ceremony
at Preston Docks.

OFFICIAL NUMBER 1155
BUILT 1989, FBM Ltd, Cowes
YARD NO 1257
DONOR Bequest of Sarah Emily Harrop, of
Harrogate, who holidayed in the Lytham St
Annes area, and had relatives living in the town
COST £589,183.58
NAMED 29.4.1990 at Preston Dock by Mrs
Edna M. Sneath

STATIONS
Lytham St Annes 14.1.1990 – 1.12.1997 (91/17)
Relief 11.1998 – 2006 (79/6)
Calshot 3.2.2007 – 21.1.2010 (161/1)
Shoreham Harbour 21.4.2010 – 11.2010 (11/0)
DISPOSAL Sold 2010 to Bere Island Ferries,
Ireland
RENAMED Ocean Lass

▲ 47-037 in Southampton Water during her three-
year stint at Calshot, January 2010. (Nicholas Leach)

▲ 47-037 at Bere Island, renamed Ocean Lass,
February 2012. (Nicholas Leach)

47-038 • William Street

47-028 on exercise at Fleetwood.

OFFICIAL NUMBER 1156
BUILT 1989, FBM Ltd, Cowes
YARD NO 1258
DONOR Trustees of W.O. Street Foundation, together with the bequests of Major Percy Frederick Holley and Francis Albert Balshaw, and a gift from Miss Hilda Richmond
COST £592,016.72

NAMED 12.5.1990 at Wyre Dock Marina, Fleetwood, by Mrs Elizabeth Acland
STATIONS
Fleetwood 15.10.1989 –30.8.2016 (536/37)
DISPOSAL Sold 2016 to Seafari Adventures, Armadale, Skye, and used, unaltered, as a work boat operating from Mallaig around the Western Isles, painted all over grey
RENAMED Amelia

▲ 47-038 returning to Fleetwood following a routine training exercise, February 1999. (Nicholas Leach)

▲ 47-038, renamed Amelia, at Mallaig as a work boat on Scotland's west coast, July 2018. (Nicholas Leach)

47-039 • Alexander Coutanche

47-039 on exercise off
Jersey, May 2007.

OFFICIAL NUMBER 1157
BUILT 1989, FBM Ltd, Cowes,
YARD NO 1259
DONOR The Jersey Lifeboat Appeal together
with a donation from the States of Jersey.
COST £592,669.78
NAMED 9.5.1990 at St Helier Marina, by Jurat
the Hon John Coutanche, son of Alexander
Coutanche, Bailiff of Jersey during WW2
STATIONS
St Helier 13.12.1989 – 14.6.2009 (408/137)

Calshot 21.1.2010 – 11.7.2012 (100/2)
Lough Swilly 12.10.2010 – 26.5.2013 (2/0)
Relief 2013 – 2014 (2/0)
DISPOSAL Sold 12.2014 to Seamus Boyle, Realt
na Maidne Teoranta of Leabgarrow, Arranmore
Island, registered in Sligo, and licenced to
carry 12 passengers; used as a work boat by
Arranmore Island Fast Ferry and in Killybegs
harbour; in 2020 she was sold to become the
Neath pilot boat, being based in Swansea
RENAMED Ocean Warrior/ Euan D

▲ 47-039 at Calshot for the station's annual Open
Day, July 2012. (Nicholas Leach)

▲ 47-039 as the pilot boat Euan D at Swansea Marina,
August 2022. (Nicholas Leach)

47-040 • Hermione Lady Colwyn

47-040 arriving at Shoreham Harbour for the first time, September 1990.

OFFICIAL NUMBER 1158

BUILT 1990, Wright, Derby/fitted out by Marshall-Branson, Amble

YARD NO 1158

DONOR Shoreham Lifeboat Appeal, and bequest of Lady Colwyn

COST £720,020.66

NAMED 29.5.1991 at Shoreham Harbour by HRH Princess Alexandra

STATIONS

Shoreham Harb 30.9.1990 – 21.4.2010 (414/39)

DISPOSAL Sold 6.2010 to Arthur Conway and became the pleasure boat Odin in Douglas Harbour; sold in June 2012 and taken to the south coast, being berthed at Berthon Marina, Lymington as the sea safety training boat Odin, later being moved to Bitterne Manor, River Itchen, in 2015; she has most recently been at East Cowes as a work boat

RENAMED Odin/Odin Nautical

▲ 47-040 following her last slipway launch at Shoreham Harbour, January 2009.

▲ 47-040 renamed Odin in the Solent, off Calshot, July 2012. (Nicholas Leach)

Map of stations served by Tynes

Map showing the stations
served by 47ft Tyne
class lifeboats.

Longhope
Wick
Fraserburgh
Peterhead
Montrose
Arranmore
Lough Swilly
Portpatrick
Hartlepool
Workington
Teesmouth
Whitby
Barrow
Douglas
Fleetwood
Lytham
St Annes
Holyhead
Moelfre
Wicklow
Cromer
Porthdinllaen
Lowestoft
Kilmore Quay
Walton and Fri
St Davids
Baltimore
Angle
Tenby
Mumbles
Ramsgate
Appledore
Calshot
Padstow
Poole
Selsey
Shoreham Harbour
Sennen Cove
Bembridge
Salcombe
Lizard
St Helier (Jersey)

TYNE FAST SLIPWAY LIFEBOATS